S0-DPG-199

MAN WALKS ON
the Moon

Written by
Douglas M. Rife

Good Apple
A Division of Frank Schaffer Publications, Inc.

Editors: Christine Hood, Kristin Eclov,
          Deborah Ross Klingsporn
Illustration: Ron Lipking
Cover Illustration: Barbara Kiwak
Cover Design and Art Direction: Jonathan Wu
Inside Design: Anthony D. Paular
Graphic Artist: Randy Shinsato

GOOD APPLE
A Division of Frank Schaffer Publications, Inc.
23740 Hawthorne Boulevard
Torrance, CA 90505

Contents

History in the Headlines Series

Surveys taken in the mid-1980s made famous the fact that American students do not like history, often ranking it as their least favorite school subject. Even tough subjects such as math were ranked higher because students saw them as more relevant than history.

Unfortunately, history has attained the reputation for being dull. Part of the reason students find history boring is that, for the most part, history textbooks tend to be lifeless, bland and uninteresting—little more than a chronological recitation of events. A long litany of what happened when, where, and with whom conveys little of the human drama that makes history a rich and colorful story.

This is not to place the blame solely on textbook companies. The development of a textbook is a long and arduous process. Textbooks are generally written by editorial committees to please curriculum adoption committees—a sure recipe for a boring book. Textbooks also rely heavily on secondary sources, which are twice removed from original accounts. Most textbooks include few primary source materials. The student is rarely introduced to firsthand accounts such as letters, diaries, newspaper articles, songs, photographs, and speeches. The text loses its narrative flow and students never get a sense of history as a great *story*, which is, after all, the root word of *history*.

History taught in this way tends not to be remembered at all. When queried, the average American student has difficulty placing events such as the American Revolution and the Civil War in the correct decade in which they occurred.

The History in the Headlines series has a two-fold purpose. The first is to focus on seminal events—those that changed the very course of American history, such as when Neil Armstrong stepped onto the surface of the moon.

In a recent survey of journalists and historians, the moon walk was listed as one of the most important events of the 20th century. From the early days of the space race, the United States came from behind. The Soviets had successfully launched *Sputnik* in 1957. Their rocket program was years ahead of the Americans. Then in May of 1961, President John F. Kennedy challenged the nation to land a man on the moon and return him safely by the end of the decade. On July 21, 1969, that goal was achieved, and the national flag was firmly planted in the soil of the moon.

Secondly, the series gives students the opportunity to read primary source material. This book includes an excerpt from a speech given by President John F. Kennedy, newspaper accounts, an editorial, editorial cartoons, and a poem that describes in sensory detail man's first steps on the moon. (Note: All handouts in this book are reproductions of actual documents. They have been printed in their original form to maintain their integrity. Any errors you may find are as they appeared in the original documents.)

Overall, the History in the Headlines series puts flesh on the skeletal histories found in basal textbooks. I hope you find it a useful supplement to your history curriculum.

The Newspaper As a Primary Source

"A newspaper is the history for one day of the world in which we live. . . ."

—George Horne

A newspaper is a snapshot of current events on a given day in history. A newspaper can be viewed as a rough draft of history and an important primary source of historical information.

Students should note, however, that not all early newspaper reports are accurate. One of the most famous examples of an embarrassing mistake is the *Chicago Daily Tribune*'s coverage of the 1948 presidential election. Based on early returns, the newspaper printed a giant banner headline on the front page that read *DEWEY DEFEATS TRUMAN*. Of course, Truman actually defeated Dewey in 1948, winning 304 electoral votes to Dewey's 189. (The popular vote was 24,105,695 to 21,969,170.) If a historian were only to focus on that one newspaper as the source of information in researching the 1948 election, he or she would come to many false conclusions, to say the least.

Like all primary sources, a newspaper story should be read with a critical eye and attention to detail. Good historians check other sources of information to corroborate facts and check the authenticity and veracity of a particular source. Historians should try to understand the motives, if any, behind the manner in which a given event is covered.

This series allows students to investigate the newspaper as a primary source of information. Students will read contemporary accounts of historical events with fresh eyes, just as the original readers did on the day the story unfolded. This series also provides students with a taste of the drama surrounding the great seminal events in American history. Finally, this series will help students read current newspapers more critically by reminding them to question and analyze what they read in these first drafts of history.

Unit Overview and Objectives

	Objectives	Critical Thinking	Activities
Excerpts From a Speech by John F. Kennedy "Freedoms Cause: These Are Extraordinary Times"	• Understand the genesis of the space race • Analyze the causes and effects of the space race • Understand the concept of primary source material	• Analyze a primary source document • Determine cause and effect relationships	• Read for comprehension • Organize data into a graphic organizer and bar graph • Conduct interviews
Los Angeles Times: **"Walk on Moon"**	• Discover the five W's and how and inverted pyramid styles of journalistic writing • Understand the basic elements of a newspaper story	• Determine the five W's and how in a newspaper article • Evaluate a news story for the most important facts	• Rewrite a news story using the inverted pyramid format • Write creative news headlines • Design a newspaper front page
Los Angeles Times: **"The Space Program Has Enriched Entire Nation In Many Ways"**	• Understand bias, fact, and fiction in news reporting • Identify and judge an editorial's opinion and point of view	• Evaluate an editorialist's point of view	• Read for comprehension • Write a newspaper editorial • Draw an editorial cartoon
Editorial Cartoons	• Understand pictorial symbolism used in editorial cartoons • Identify and judge a cartoonist's message • Recognize the use of humor and stereotypes in editorial cartoons	• Evaluate editorial cartoons and form opinions • Draw inferences using visual clues	• Restate a cartoonist's message in own words • Draw an editorial cartoon
Literature Connection: "First Walk on the Moon"	• Interpret symbolism in a poem • Identify characteristics of metaphor and onomatopoeia	• Evaluate a poem for poetic conventions	• Evaluate a poem for meaning, poetic conventions, and symbolism

A Speech by President John F. Kennedy
"Freedom's Cause:
These Are Extraordinary Times"

Objectives
- Understand the genesis of the space race
- Analyze the causes and effects of the space race
- Understand the concept of primary source material

Vocabulary

Satellite: An object that travels around another object in space

Sputnik: The Soviet Union launched a series of satellites named *Sputnik* from 1957 to 1961, beginning with the first on October 4, 1957. Though this 184-pound satellite fell to Earth on January 4, 1958, only 92 days later, it represented a dramatic lead in the space race for the Soviets.

Background

After the humiliation of the Soviet launch of *Sputnik,* the space race was on. The Americans did not want to come in second in a two-horse, or rather, "two rocket," race to space. In 1958, the United States organized a civilian space agency (NASA) to catch up with the Soviets. This space agency had four justifications for its development—man's curiosity, national defense, national prestige, and scientific growth. Clearly, the United States did not want to be seen as behind the Soviets technologically, especially during the height of the Cold War.

Who's Who

Alan Shepard

On May 5, 1961, Shepard was launched into space in a Redstone rocket inside a capsule named *Freedom 7.* The flight lasted 15 minutes and propelled Shepard 116 miles into the atmosphere at 5,180 miles per hour.

President John F. Kennedy

Kennedy was elected president in 1960 in a very close election with Richard Nixon. Kennedy had served in the House of Representatives and the Senate.

Vice President Lyndon B. Johnson

As Democratic majority leader of the Senate, Johnson is credited with drafting the legislation that created NASA in 1958. Lyndon B. Johnson was elected vice president in 1960, and succeeded to the presidency in 1963 after John F. Kennedy was assassinated.

Suggested Lesson Plan

1. Display the newspaper poster from the inside of the book in your classroom. This will help introduce the topic of the moon walk to the class.

2. As a homework assignment, you may have students interview their parents about their memories of the moon landing. Invite students to share these stories with the class.

3. Explain lesson objectives to the students. Review the lesson vocabulary and background information.

4. Distribute the "Freedoms Cause" handout (pages 9 and 10). Read and discuss the speech with students. This is an excerpt from a speech given before a joint session of Congress, May 25, 1961, by President John F. Kennedy, just 20 days after the first successful U.S. manned space flight. The title of the speech is "Freedoms Cause: These Are Extraordinary Times." This speech is seen by many historians as the speech that began the United States–Soviet space race. This space race became an integral part of the Cold War.

5. Distribute the "Space Race" activity sheets (pages 11 and 12). Go over these pages with students, and encourage them to complete the activities individually or in small groups.

Freedom's Cause:
These Are Extraordinary Times

Finally, if we are to win the battle that is going on around the world between freedom and tyranny, if we are to win the battle for men's minds, the dramatic achievements in space which occurred in recent weeks should have made clear to us all, as did the sputnik in 19[5]7, the impact of this adventure on the minds of men everywhere who are attempting to make a determination of which road they should take. Since early in my term our efforts in space have been under review. With the advice of the Vice President, who is Chairman of the National Space Council, we have examined where we are strong and where we are not. Now it is time to take longer strides—time for a great new American enterprise—time for this Nation to take a clearly leading role in space achievement which in many ways may hold the key to our future on earth.

I believe we possess all the resources and all the talents necessary. But the facts of the matter are that we have never made the national decisions or marshaled the national resources required for such leadership. We have never specified long-range goals on an urgent time schedule, or managed our resources and our time so as to insure their fulfillment.

Recognizing the head start obtained by the Soviets with their large rocket engines, which gives them many months of leadtime, and recognizing the likelihood that they will exploit this lead for some time to come in still more impressive successes, we nevertheless are required to make new efforts on our own. For while we cannot guarantee that we shall one day be first, we can guarantee that any failure to make this effort will find us last. We take an additional risk by making it in full view of the world—but as shown by the feat of Astronaut Shepard, this very risk enhances our stature when we are successful. But this is not merely a race. Space is open to us now; and our eagerness to share its meaning is not governed by the efforts of others. We go into space because whatever mankind must undertake, freeman must fully share.

I therefore ask the Congress, above and beyond the increases I have earlier requested for space activities, to provide the funds which are needed to meet the following national goals:

First, I believe that this Nation should commit itself to achieving the goal, before this decade is out, of landing a man on the moon and returning him safely to earth. No single space project in this period will be more exciting, or more impressive to mankind, or more important for the long-range exploration of space; and none will be so difficult or expensive to accomplish. Including necessary supporting research, this objective will require an additional $531 million this year and still higher sums in the future. We propose to accelerate development of the appropriate lunar spacecraft. We propose to develop alternate liquid and solid fuel boosters much larger than any now being developed, until certain which is superior. We propose additional funds for other engine development and for unmanned explorations—explorations which are particularly important for one purpose which this Nation will never overlook; the survival of the man who first makes this daring flight. But in a very real sense, it will not be one man going to the moon—we make this judgment affirmatively—it will be an entire nation. For all of us must work to put him there.

Continued on page 10

Continued from page 9

Second, an additional $23 million, together with $7 million already available, will accelerate development of the ROVER nuclear rocket. This is a technological enterprise in which we are well on the way to striking progress, and which gives promise of some day providing a means for even more exciting and ambitious exploration of space, perhaps beyond the moon, perhaps to the very ends of the solar system itself.

Third, an additional $50 million will make the most of our present leadership by accelerating the use of space satellites for worldwide communications. When we have put into space a system that will enable people in remote areas of the earth to exchange messages, hold conversations, and eventually see television programs, we will have achieved a success as beneficial as it will be striking.

Fourth, an additional $75 million—of which $53 million is for the Weather Bureau—will help give us at the earliest possible time a satellite system for worldwide weather observation. Such a system will be of inestimable commercial and scientific value; and the information it provides will be made freely available to all the nations of the world.

Let it be clear—and this is a judgment which the Members of the Congress must finally make—let it be clear that I am asking the Congress and the country to accept a firm commitment to a new course of action—a course which will last for many years and carry very heavy costs, $531 million in the fiscal year 1962 and an estimated $7–9 billion additional over the next 5 years. If we are to go only halfway, or reduce our sights in the face of difficulty, in my judgment it would be better not to go at all. This is the choice which this country must make, and I am confident that under the leadership of the Space committees of the Congress and the appropriations committees you will consider the matter carefully. It is a most important decision that we make as a nation; but all of you have lived through the last 4 years and have seen the significance of space and the adventures in space, and no one can predict with any certainty what the ultimate meaning will be of the mastery of space. I believe we should go to the moon. But I think every citizen of this country as well as the Members of Congress should consider the matter carefully in making their judgment, to which we have given attention over many weeks and months, as it is a heavy burden; and there is no sense in agreeing, or desiring, that the United States take an affirmative position in outer space unless we are prepared to do the work and bear the burdens to make it successful. If we are not, we should decide today.

Let me stress also that more money alone will not do the job. This decision demands a major national commitment of scientific and technical manpower, material and facilities, and the possibility of their diversion from other important activities where they are already thinly spread. It means a degree of dedication, organization, and discipline which have not always characterized our research and development efforts. It means we cannot afford undue work stoppages, inflated costs of material or talent, wasteful interagency rivalries, or a high turnover of key personnel.

Excerpted from "Freedom's Cause: These Are Extraordinary Times," a speech by President John F. Kennedy, May 25, 1961.

Space Race

Chart 1: NASA Expenditures for Research and Development (1961–1970)

Billions of Dollars

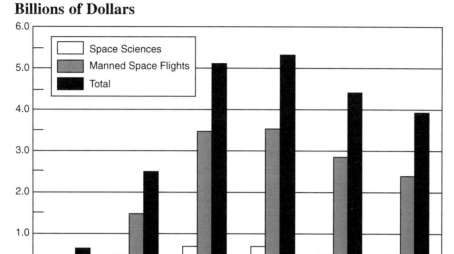

Chart 2: Comparison of U.S. and Soviet Space Launchings, Military and Civilian (1957–1968)

	Rockets Sent into Space for Civil Reasons				Military Rockets	
Year	NASA	DoD	U.S. Total	U.S.S.R.	DoD	U.S.S.R.
1957	0	0	0	2	0	0
1958	0	5	5	1	0	0
1959	5	0	5	3	5	0
1960	5	1	6	3	10	0
1961	10	0	10	6	19	0
1962	18	1	19	15	33	5
1963	10	2	12	10	26	7
1964	22	2	24	17	33	13
1965	23	9	32	24	31	24
1966	30	9	39	20	34	24
1967	25	6	31	29	26	37
1968	19	4	23	32	22	42
Totals	**167**	**39**	**206**	**162**	**239**	**152**

DoD = The United States Department of Defense

NASA = National Aeronautics and Space Agency

USSR = The Union of Soviet Socialist Republics

Name_____

Space Race

Many historians would argue that the successful Soviet launch of *Sputnik 1* triggered the United States' efforts in space. Use the graphic organizer below to list several causes and effects of the space race. You do not have to match causes and effects.

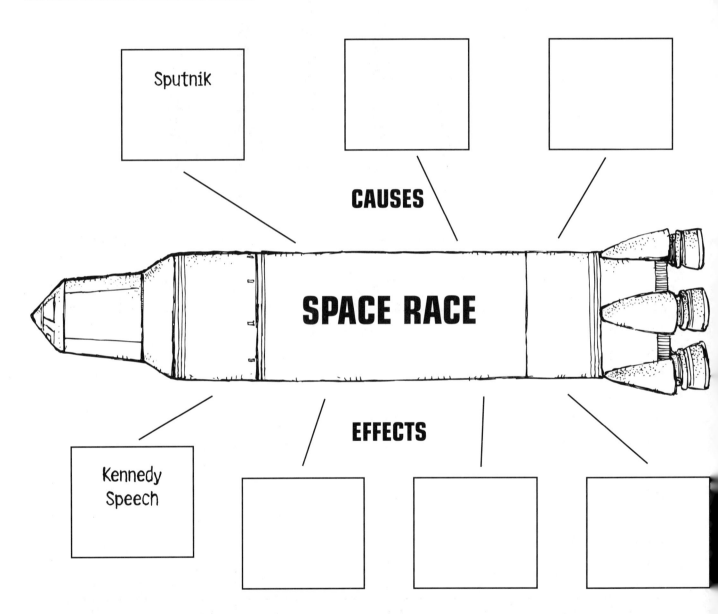

Extension Activity

Using the data from Chart 2 on page 11, create a bar graph showing the number of U.S. civilian rockets, Soviet civilian rockets, U.S. military rockets, and Soviet military rockets.

Los Angeles Times
"Walk on Moon"

Objectives

- Discover the five W's and how and inverted pyramid styles of journalistic writing
- Understand the basic elements of a newspaper story

Vocabulary

Lead: The first and most important paragraph in a newspaper article. In many cases the reader will get no further than the first paragraph, so it is vital that this paragraph carry the most important facts of the news story.

Middle Paragraphs: The information in the paragraphs following the lead should contain important supporting information. These are facts a reader will want to read, but in the hierarchy of the story, these paragraphs carry facts less important than in the lead.

Ending Paragraphs: These paragraphs have the least bearing on the story. They explain more relevant facts to the story but are written so that any of them could be cut without losing the most important facts.

Who's Who

Three astronauts are mentioned in the story—Neil A. Armstrong, Edwin E. Aldrin, Jr., and Michael Collins. **Neil Armstrong** was born in 1930 in Wapakoneta, Ohio. Armstrong graduated from Purdue University. He was a Navy pilot and a test pilot when he joined NASA as an astronaut. Armstrong was the first person in history to set foot on the moon. **Edwin Aldrin, Jr.,** was the second American to step onto the moon. Aldrin was also born in 1930, in Montclair, New Jersey. Aldrin was a graduate of the U.S. Military Academy. He served in the Korean War as a pilot. After he received his doctorate in astronautics from MIT in 1963, he joined NASA. **Michael Collins**, the son of a U.S. Army serviceman, was born in 1930 in Rome, Italy. Collins was a graduate of the U.S. Military Academy in 1952. Afterward, he served as an Air Force officer. In 1966, Collins joined NASA.

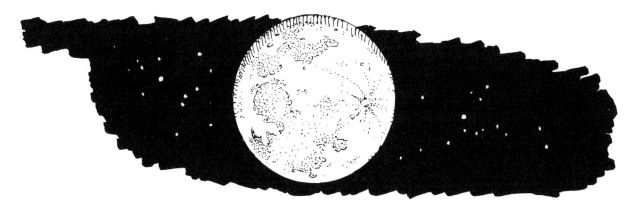

Background

In newspaper writing, the philosophy is to get the most important information in the lead paragraph of the news story. This journalistic form of writing, called the inverted pyramid, was popularized in newspapers in the 1920s. The theory is that many people never read past the first paragraph, so this paragraph should carry the most important information. The paragraphs that follow carry supporting information, and the last paragraphs carry news that still supports the lead but could be cut if the story runs long. The foundation is upside down. Good news stories also answer questions readers want to know—*who, what, when, where, why,* and *how.* These elements, which should be included in every good story, are called the five W's and how.

Suggested Lesson Plan

1. Discuss lesson objectives with students, as well as lesson vocabulary and background information.
2. Distribute the "Walk on Moon" handout (pages 15 and 16). Read and discuss the article with students. Point out that every good news story includes the five W's and how.
3. Ask students to clip newspaper stories and identify how quickly the five-W's-and-how questions are answered in the stories.
4. Distribute the activity sheets (pages 17–19). Encourage students to evaluate the "Walk on Moon" newspaper article for journalistic writing style and format. Then have them complete the activity sheets. When students create their own newspaper front pages, you may want to have them work in groups, creating real stories, taking real photographs, and creating interesting fonts on the computer.

Los Angeles Times
WALK ON MOON
'That's One Small Step for Man...
One Giant Leap for Mankind'

Armstrong Beams His Words to Earth After Testing Surface

BY MARVIN MILES and
RUDY ABRAMSON

Times Staff Writers

HOUSTON—U.S. astronauts stepped onto the surface of the moon Sunday and explored its bleak, forbidding crust in man's first visit to another celestial body.

Apollo 11 Commander Neil A. Armstrong climbed slowly down the ladder from the spaceship Eagle, and became the first man to set foot on the lunar surface.

As Armstrong swung his left boot to the surface of the moon at 7:56 p.m., PDT, he gave millions of spellbound television viewers words sure to live in history:

"That's one small step for man . . . one giant leap for mankind."

Nearly seven hours earlier, Armstrong had averted possible disaster by taking full manual control of the vehicle on landing, selecting a safe spot for man's first landing on the moon.

Much of the civilized world watched and listened as Armstrong and fellow explorer Edwin E. Aldrin Jr., who followed him down the steps about 20 minutes later, collected rocks which may reveal the oldest secrets of the solar system.

Collins Waits, Listens

Waiting and listening in lunar orbit was the third member of the Apollo crew, command module pilot Michael Collins.

As he took his first steps on the lunar surface, Armstrong could be seen in remarkably clear television pictures taken by a camera attached to the lunar module descent stage. He described what he found.

He said the surface "appears fine-grained, almost like a powder. I can kick it up loosely with my foot. I only go in maybe an eighth of an inch."

Armstrong said the lunar module's round footpads penetrated the surface only one to two inches.

At first the black-and-white pictures were silhouettes, but then as Armstrong moved away from the ladder his bulky life support pack could be discerned. In almost no time Armstrong was moving around the surface rapidly—quickly adapting to the lunar environment.

The spacecraft commander went to work on his first major assignment, the gathering of a contingency sample of lunar soil. This is a "quick grab" of sample material, about two pounds, retrieved with a butterfly net-type device.

The contingency sample was planned to assure that at least some lunar material would be brought back to earth if for any reason the astronauts had to launch from the moon in an emergency.

At one point he said he had penetrated the surface six to eight inches with the sampler and told Mission Control, "I'm sure I could push it in further."

Continued On page 16

Continued from page 15

Practices Several Jumps

Aldrin was down on the surface of the moon at 8:16 p.m. with an athletic drop of what appeared to be about three feet. He then immediately practiced several jumps to determine the effect of the moon's weight gravity on his balance and coordination.

Mission Control here asked Armstrong if he foresaw any difficulty transferring equipment back and forth between the surface and the lunar module cabin in the top stage of the spacecraft and his cryptic reply was "Negative."

As soon as Aldrin was on the surface, both men could be seen by the television audience working near the ladder which was mounted on the lander's forward leg.

One of the first tasks of the two men after Armstrong gathered the contingency sample and stowed it in a bag in his spacesuit pocket, was to make a cursory examination of his spacecraft, particularly its landing legs and shocks. He had some trouble in stowing the sample because the suit, bulky with many layers of material and 35 pounds per square inch pressurization, was stiff and he could not tell if the pocket was open. He had to ask for Aldrin's assistance.

Aldrin's first comment after reaching the surface was that the rocks felt quite "slippery."

Both astronauts wore their heavy gold sunshields pulled down over their fishbowl helmets and their faces could not be discerned.

In no time it seemed that both men were acclimated entirely to the lunar environment, as they moved around with ease, flung their arms and legs and jumped as if in happiness but actually in tests of mobility.

At one juncture Aldrin reported, "I was about to lose my balance in one direction but recovery is quite natural."

Early in the moon walk there was not too much description of the landing scene itself except Armstrong's note: "It's different but beautiful."

While Aldrin worked at an equipment bay in the module's lower stage, removing tools and rockboxes, Armstrong moved out to one side of the lander, perhaps 60 or 70 feet, then aimed the camera in a series of panoramic views of the area.

Desolation Shown

The scene showed clearly the utter desolation of the moon—the rough, scarred terrain, in what appeared to be scores of small craters. The pictures showed a couple of elongated craters, and in the distance small rocks.

Once he had fixed the camera on the tripod, Armstrong moved back to center stage where Aldrin was busy mounting a solar wind detector, something like a windowblind to catch particles of the solar wind for return to earth.

Over and over again, the explorers noted the cohesiveness of the moon's soil.

From early moments of their explorations, physicians in Mission Control reported the pilots remained in excellent physical condition.

No Indications

There were no indications in their voices that they were excited, confused or fatigued by the physical and emotional experience.

Aldrin said his blue lunar overshoes had turned to a grayish cocoa color after his striding about for a time in the lunar dust.

Forty-five minutes after Armstrong stepped down from the ladder onto the surface, the two pilots planted the American Flag just in front of the lander.

The Flag was carried to the moon in a container along side the ladder. Mounted on an eight foot staff, it was held out by a spring, making it look almost as though it were in a stiff breeze.

Excerpted from "Walk on Moon," *Los Angeles Times*, July 21, 1969. Reprinted with permission.

EXTF

COMPLETE RACING

Los Ange

LARGEST CIRCULATION IN THE

VOL. LXXXVIII   FIVE PARTS—PART ONE   MONDAY

WALK OI

'That's One Sma

One Giant Lea

TAKING A WALK—Neil A. Armstrong, wearing life-support backpack, steps on lunar surface after

PLANTING THE FLAG—Armstrong and Edwin E. Aldrin Jr. setting Stars and Stripes on the moon.

RA

s Times

MONDAY

FINAL

ILY, 1,308,711 SUNDAY.

JULY 21, 1969   84 PAGES   Copyright © 1969
Los Angeles Times   DAILY 10c

MOON

Step for Man...
for Mankind'

Armstrong Beams His Words to Earth After Testing Surface

BY MARVIN MILES and RUDY ABRAMSON
Times Staff Writers

HOUSTON—U.S. astronauts stepped onto the surface of the moon Sunday and explored its bleak, forbidding crust in man's first visit to another celestial body.

Apollo 11 Commander Neil A. Armstrong climbed slowly down the ladder from the spaceship Eagle, and became the first man to set foot

time Armstrong was moving around the surface rapidly—quickly adapting to the lunar environment

on the lunar surface.

As Armstrong swung his left boot to the surface of the moon at 7:56 p.m., PDT, he gave millions of spellbound television viewers words sure to live in history:

"That's one small step for man . . . one giant leap for mankind."

Nearly seven hours earlier, Armstrong had averted possible disaster by taking full manual control of the vehicle on landing, selecting a safe spot for man's first landing on the moon.

Much of the c i v i l i z e d world watched and listened as Armstrong and fellow explorer Edwin E. Aldrin Jr., who followed him down the steps about 20 minutes later, collected rocks which may reveal the oldest secrets of the solar system.

Collins Waits, Listens

Waiting and listening in lunar orbit was the third member of the Apollo crew, command module pilot Michael Collins.

As he took his first steps on the lunar surface, Armstrong could be seen in remarkably clear television pictures taken by a camera attached to the lunar module descent stage. He described what he found.

He said the surface "appears fine-grained, almost like a powder. I can kick it up loosely with my foot. I only go in maybe an eighth of an inch."

Armstrong said the lunar module's round footpads penetrated the surface only one to two inches.

At first the black-and-white pictures were silhouettes, but then as Armstrong moved away from the ladder his bulky life support pack could be discerned. In almost no

ladder of the spacecraft.

ht, left, is a landing leg.
UPI Wirephotos

The spacecraft commander went to work on his first major assignment, the gathering of a contingency sample of lunar soil. This is a "quick grab" of sample material, about two pounds, retrieved with a butterfly net-type device.

The contingency s a m p l e w a s planned to assure that at least some lunar material would be brought back to earth if for any reason the astronauts had to launch from the moon in an emergency.

At one point he said he had penetrated the surface six to eight inches with the sampler and told Mission Control, "I'm sure I could push it in further."

Practices Several Jumps

Aldrin was down on the surface of the moon at 8:16 p.m. with an athletic drop of what appeared to be about three feet. He then immediately practiced several jumps to determine the effect of the moon's weight gravity on his balance and coordination.

Mission Control here asked Armstrong if he foresaw any difficulty transferring equipment back and forth between the surface and the lunar module cabin in the top stage of the spacecraft and his cryptic reply was "Negative."

As soon as Aldrin was on the surface, both men could be seen by the television audience working near the ladder which was mounted on the lander's forward leg.

One of the first tasks of the two men after Armstrong gathered the contingency sample and stowed it in a bag in his spacesuit pocket, was to

Please Turn to Page 10, Col. 1

TALKS TO ASTRONAUTS

Heavens Have Become Part of Man's World, Nixon Says

WASHINGTON — For two minutes Sunday night, President Nixon spoke via radiotelephone to his farthest flung countrymen—American astronauts in the moon's Sea of Tranquility—and told them:

"Because of what you have done, the heavens have become part of man's world and, as you talk to us from the Sea of Tranquility, it inspires us to redouble our efforts to bring peace and tranquility to the earth."

Those were the official words of the President of the United States, speaking from the august Oval Office of the White House.

A few minutes earlier, Mr. Nixon, like television viewers all over the world, sat in a smaller, private, more informal office and watched astronaut Neil A. Armstrong climb down from his moon landing ship to set the first human feet on the moon.

The President, his eyes fixed on the set, said:

"It's an unbelievable thing. Fantastic."

Col. Frank Borman, who commanded the Apollo 8 Christmastime voyage around the moon, was with the President when Armstrong took his walk. He provided the President with a running commentary and explained the technicalities of the mission.

Why, Mr. Nixon wanted to know,

Please Turn to Page 8, Col. 3

Name_____

Journalistic Writing Styles

Inverted Pyramid

Read the article on the "Walk on Moon" handout. Rewrite the story using the inverted pyramid format below. List only the basic facts. Then on another sheet of paper, draw a full-size pyramid in which to write your entire story.

Lead _____

_____

_____

Middle _____

_____

_____

Ending _____

_____

_____

The Five W's and How

The information in every good news story is basically the same: Who is the story about? What happened? When did it happen? Where did it happen? Why did it happen? How did it happen? Read the article "Walk on Moon." Then answer the questions below.

Who? _____

What? _____

When? _____

Where? _____

Why? _____

How? _____

Name_____

Newspaper Headlines

Headlines grab the reader's attention and help sell newspapers. They are often the most difficult part of a story to write. Headlines can be written many different ways, including humorously, as a celebration, or sincerely. A headline often tries to tell the most important part of a story in one awe-inspiring statement; it may shock, celebrate, mourn, or incite anger. Whatever the purpose behind the headline, it is meant to grab the reader's attention and encourage him or her to read on.

Read the article "Walk on Moon." Write three serious headlines that would grab the reader's attention.

1. _____

2. _____

3. _____

Write three humorous headlines that would grab the reader's attention.

1. _____

2. _____

3. _____

Which headline do you think would attract the most attention? Why?

_____

_____

_____

_____

Extension Activity

Write an essay comparing Neil Armstrong and Edwin E. Aldrin, Jr., to Meriwether Lewis and William Clark. How were their missions the same? How were their missions different? Compare the equipment, the distance of each exploration, and the time each mission took.

The Front Page

Look over all the elements in the sample newspaper front page below. Then create your own newspaper front page on a large sheet of butcher paper. Make sure to include all the elements, including interesting photographs and art.

The Good Apple Gazette

Ear
a box on either side of the flag, usually containing weather information

Banner
top headline on page one

Caption
copy above a photograph

Byline
credit to a reporter or writer of a story

Dateline
place where story originated

Credit Line
name of photographer

Art
art on the page of any kind—photo, illustration, or chart

Cutline
copy below a photograph

Box
story appearing inside a box or under a bar or line

Folio
page number

Flag
name of the newspaper

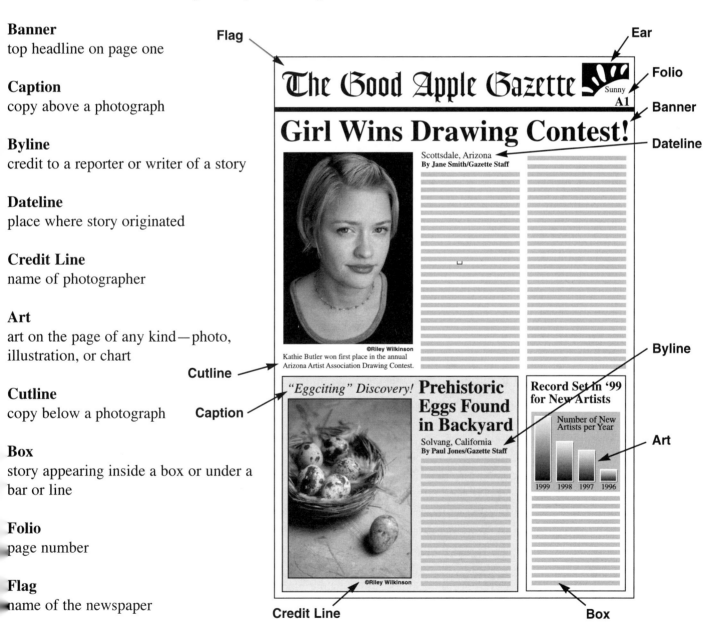

Flag · Ear · Folio · Banner · Dateline · Byline · Art · Box · Credit Line · Caption · Cutline

The Good Apple Gazette
Sunny
A1

Girl Wins Drawing Contest!

Scottsdale, Arizona
By Jane Smith/Gazette Staff

©Riley Wilkinson
Kathie Butler won first place in the annual Arizona Artist Association Drawing Contest.

"Eggciting" Discovery! **Prehistoric Eggs Found in Backyard**

Solvang, California
By Paul Jones/Gazette Staff

©Riley Wilkinson

Record Set in '99 for New Artists

Number of New Artists per Year

1999 1998 1997 1996

Los Angeles Times
"Space Program Has Enriched Entire Nation in Many Ways"

Objectives
- Understand bias, fact, and fiction in news reporting
- Identify and judge an editorial's opinion and point of view

Vocabulary

Red: Of or related to the Soviet Union

Space Age: The dawn of the "Space Age" is considered to begin on the date the Soviets launched *Sputnik 1* on October 4, 1957. This age is characterized by humankind's exploration of space and man-made objects being sent into space—manned and unmanned.

Background

Hubert Humphrey

Humphrey was a longtime U.S. Senator from Minnesota. Humphrey was elected to the vice presidency in 1964, and served under Lyndon B. Johnson. He was defeated in 1968 by Richard Nixon for the presidency. After his defeat, he was re-elected to the Senate to represent, once again, the state of Minnesota. The following editorial appeared in the *Los Angeles Times* on Monday, July 21, 1969, the day the astronauts landed on the moon. As the reader can tell from the article, the astronauts had not yet returned, and there was apprehension about their return. Humphrey was a longtime supporter of the space program.

Suggested Lesson Plan

1. Explain lesson objectives to students. Review the lesson vocabulary and background information.
2. Distribute the "Space Program Has Enriched Entire Nation in Many Ways" handout (pages 21 and 22). Read and discuss the editorial with students, including questions such as: *What are some arguments that the writer uses to convince the reader of his point of view?* (1. Communication satellites have revolutionized worldwide communication; 2. The space program has upgraded American industry and management; 3. Space exploration has promoted international cooperation.) Ask students to express their opinions. Do they think the editorial is convincing?
3. Have students complete the "Editorial Evaluation" activity sheet (page 23).
4. As an extension, have students write their own editorials about the space program. Students can also draw editorial cartoons illustrating Humphrey's point of view.

𝕷𝖔𝖘 𝕬𝖓𝖌𝖊𝖑𝖊𝖘 𝕿𝖎𝖒𝖊𝖘
Space Program Has Enriched Entire Nation in Many Ways

BY HUBERT H. HUMPHREY

MOSCOW—On Oct. 4, 1957, a new star appeared in the sky—the red star of the Soviet Union, the red star of Sputnik.

I remember the shock that spread across America when we realized that the Russians were first in space, and with a much larger satellite than the planned U.S. Vanguard. We realized that the competition from the Soviet Union was much tougher than we had anticipated—not only in ideology, but also in technology.

Congress reacted with the National Aeronautics and Space Act of 1958. The then-majority leader of the Senate, Lyndon B. Johnson, was largely responsible for drafting the act and enacting it into law. Since then, Congress has approved a total investment in space of $50 billion, with $24 billion of it for the Apollo program.

If the Apollo 11 flight goes well from beginning to end, we will have fulfilled President John F. Kennedy's commitment that in this decade we land a man on the moon and return him safely to earth, and

we unquestionably will be the world leader in space exploration and technology.

I am now in the Soviet Union, the nation that triggered our massive space effort. I will emphasize to the Russians that the commemorative plaque to be left on the moon—"We came in peace for all mankind"—expresses our hopes that space exploration will benefit all people.

In America, the space program has been hotly debated. The question is asked: Has space been given too high a priority? The flight of Apollo 11 is full of drama, but could the money be better spent to rebuild our cities?

For four years as Vice President, I served as chairman of the National Aeronautics and Space Council. The council coordinated our space program, and I visited our space centers and got to know our scientists.

I am convinced that our space program is a wise investment in the future. If you look behind the fanfare of the space flights, you will see, as I have, the steady and

significant contributions of our space program to education, medicine, communications, weather forecasting and the whole range of technological development—electronics, computers, metallurgy and more.

We have trained thousands of scientists under space grants. Almost $800 million has been distributed directly to colleges and universities under the space program. These grants have helped to break down the compartmentalization of our universities—there is now more interdisciplinary cooperation.

Without the space program, there would be no communications satellites, which are revolutionizing worldwide communications and which will help make education available to people in every area of the world.

The space program, more than any other single development, has upgraded American industry and management. In fact, the space program is just another name for excellence in American technology.

Continued on page 22

Continued from page 21

Our mastery of space has contributed significantly to our national security and, beyond that, has opened the skies to allow the kind of inspection that will have to accompany arms control agreements.

Space exploration has promoted international co-operation—the best minds of different nations are working together to solve common problems. If we pursue this opportunity, we can work with the Soviet Union and other nations in the peaceful exploration of outer space.

Earth resource satellites can help us feed the people of earth. These satellites will find water to make the deserts bloom. They can detect disease in crops. They can find schools of fish and discover new mineral deposits.

Perhaps most important of all, our voyage to the moon has shown us that if we make a commitment and work together, we can do almost anything.

We must make a similar commitment to rebuild our cities, to clean up our air and water, to provide quality education and health care to all of our people.

Finally, our space program has given us pride and confidence as a people. Man does not live by bread alone. Our space achievements represent more than just wealth and power. They are testimony to the quality of our people. Our astronauts grew up in America, and they represent the hopes and aspirations of all the American people.

So the space program is more than just adventure, scientific miracles, expensive hardware and costly experimentation. It has enriched all of us, and someday it will carry us into our neighborhood of tomorrow—the solar system.

Copyright © *Los Angeles Times*. Reprinted with permission.

Name_____

Editorial Evaluation

1. Who is the editorialist?

_____

2. What was his position in the government?

_____

_____

3. List six industries and institutions Humphrey claims the space program has helped.

_____

_____

_____

_____

_____

_____

4. List five contributions Humphrey claims the space program has made to the nation.

_____

_____

_____

_____

_____

Extension Activities

- Write an editorial expressing your opinion about funding the space program today. In your editorial, touch on the differences or similarities, based on your viewpoint, between needs for the space program today compared to the 1960s.
- Research one of the industries Humphrey claims the space program has helped, and write an essay on how these contributions of the space program have helped Americans' everyday life.

Editorial Cartoons

Objectives

- Understand pictorial symbolism used in editorial cartoons
- Recognize the use of humor and stereotypes in editorial cartoons
- Identify and judge a cartoonist's message and point of view

Vocabulary

Caricature: A drawing of a person with exaggerated features

Editorial Cartoon: A drawing, often with a caption, that illustrates an opinion on a current issue

Symbolism: In editorial cartoons, art (symbol) is used to illustrate or represent (symbolize) an idea, person, country, and so on.

Background

Cartoonists convey their opinions using art rather than words. Even though most editorial cartoons contain some text—usually just a caption—most of the message is found in the art. The cartoonist expects the reader to understand the message conveyed in the illustration. The cartoonist must use familiar symbols and caricatures to relate his or her message about the event being editorialized.

Suggested Lesson Plan

1. Explain the lesson objectives to students. Review the lesson vocabulary and background information. Explain that editorial cartoons are opinions, just like written editorials, only they are expressed through illustration.

2. Have students complete the editorial cartoon activity sheets (pages 25–27). Invite students to study each cartoon, thinking about how each relates to and expresses an opinion about the space program.

3. Have students draw their own editorial cartoons to express their opinions about the space program or an issue or event currently in the news.

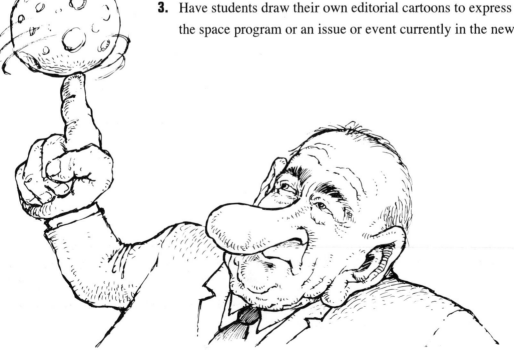

Name_____

"... And a Boomerang ..."

This cartoon appeared in the *Los Angeles Times* on July 19, 1969, two days before Neil Armstrong stepped on the moon. Study the cartoon and complete each statement by writing the correct letter on the line.

Copyright © July 19, 1969, by the *Los Angeles Times*. Reprinted with permission.

...And a Boomerang...

1. _____ The man in the cartoon is:
   a. Neil Armstrong
   b. Richard Nixon
   c. Uncle Sam
   d. Nikita Khrushchev

2. _____ The man in the space helmet is a symbol of:
   a. astronauts
   b. the presidency
   c. the United States
   d. none of the above

3. _____ The man in the cartoon is carrying:
   a. a rolled-up scroll.
   b. a baton
   c. a short stick
   d. all of the above

4. _____ The hammer and sickle represents:
   a. the Soviet Union
   b. Uruguay
   c. Uganda
   d. the United States

5. _____ The man in the cartoon is:
   a. trying to get to the moon first
   b. worried about the competition
   c. running a race
   d. all of the above

6. _____ The cartoon uses:
   a. humor to make its point
   b. satire to make its point
   c. ridicule to make its point
   d. none of the above

Extension Activity

On another sheet of paper, explain how the cartoon relates to John F. Kennedy's speech "Freedom's Cause: These Are Extraordinary Times."

Name_____

"Beyond Comfortable Horizons"

This cartoon first ran in the *Los Angeles Times* on July 21, 1969, the morning the astronauts first walked on the moon. Study the cartoon and complete each statement by writing the correct letter on the line.

Copyright © July 21, 1969, by the *Los Angeles Times*.
Reprinted with permission.

1. _____ The couple in the cartoon is:
   a. talking at the breakfast table
   b. discussing the news of the day
   c. still dressed in their robes
   d. all of the above

2. _____ The cartoonist portrays the couple as:
   a. concerned citizens
   b. apathetic Americans
   c. fascinated about the *Apollo 11* landing on the moon
   d. none of the above

3. _____ The cartoonist uses satire to portray:
   a. the plight of the average American
   b. more important concerns of average Americans
   c. an average couple discussing the news
   d. none of the above

4. _____ According to the cartoon, the couple is concerned about:
   a. gun legislation
   b. rising inflation
   c. the *Apollo 11* landing
   d. all of the above

5. In your own words, explain what the cartoon means.

_____

_____

_____

_____

reproducible　　　　　　　　　**26**

Name_____

"I Suppose It Was Inevitable!"

This cartoon first appeared in the *Los Angeles Times* on Friday, July 25, 1969. Study the cartoon and answer the following questions.

Copyright © July 25, 1969, by the *Los Angeles Times*. Reprinted with permission.

"I suppose it was inevitable!"–

1. What is the man selling in the cartoon?

_____

2. Describe how the man in the cartoon is portrayed by the cartoonist.

_____

_____

3. Explain how stereotyping plays a part of this cartoon.

_____

_____

4. Do you think the two women in the cartoon are interested in buying moon rocks from the man? Explain your answer.

_____

_____

5. What message is the cartoon sending about selling in America?

_____

_____

6. Explain whether or not you agree with the cartoonist, and why.

_____

_____

_____

"First Walk on the Moon"

Objectives
- Interpret symbolism in a poem
- Identify characteristics of metaphor and onomatopoeia

Vocabulary

Free Verse: A form of poetry with no set pattern of rhythm, meter, or rhyme

> **Example:**
> "Fog" by Carl Sandburg
> The fog comes
> On little cat feet
> It sits looking
> Over harbor and city
> On silent haunches
> And then moves on.

Metaphor: An implied comparison between two unlike things

> **Examples:**
> This place is a zoo!
> My home is my castle!

Onomatopoeia: A literary form in which words sound like their meaning, such as *snap, hiss, thud*

Background

May Swenson (1919–1989)

Swenson was born in Logan, Utah. Swenson worked as an editor in New York; as a writer in residence at Purdue University; the University of North Carolina; Lothbridge University; and the University of California, Riverside. She wrote poetry for 50 years; her first poems were published in 1949. She was known for writing poetry that used vivid imagery and unconventional punctuation and form. She was best known for her shape poems. She was often compared to Emily Dickinson.

Suggested Lesson Plan

1. Explain lesson objectives to students, and review lesson vocabulary and background information.
2. Distribute the "First Walk on the Moon" handout (page 29). Read and discuss the poem with students.
3. Distribute the "First Walk on the Moon" activity sheet (page 30). You may use this activity as a class discussion starter, or have students answer questions individually or in small groups.

First Walk on the Moon

(1) Ahead, the sun's face in a flaring hood,
was wearing the moon, a mask of shadow
that stood between. Cloudy earth
waned, gibbous, while our target grew:
an occult bloom, until it lay beneath
the fabricated insect we flew. Pitched
out of orbit we yawed in, to impact
softly on that circle.

(2) Not "ground"
the footpads found for traction.
So, far, we haven't the name.
So call it "terrain," pitted and pocked
to the round horizon (which looked
too near): a slope of rubble where
protuberant cones, dish-shaped hollows,
great sockets glared, half blind
with shadow, and smaller sucked-in folds
squinted, like blowholes on a scape
of whales.

(3) Rigid and pneumatic, we
emerged, white twin uniforms on the dark
"mare," our heads transparent spheres,
the outer visors gold. The light was
glacier bright, our shadows long,
thin fissures, of "ink." We felt neither
hot nor cold.

(4) Our boot cleats sank
into "grit, something like glass,"
but sticky. Our tracks remain
on what was virgin "soil." But that's
not the name.

(5) There was no air there,
no motion, no sound outside our heads.
We brought what we breathed
on our backs: the square papooses we
carried were our life sacks. We spoke
in numbers, fed the ratatattat of data
to amplified earth. We saw no spore
that any had stepped before us. Not
a thing has been born here, and nothing
has died, we thought.

(6) We had practiced
to walk, but we toddled (with caution,
ambition make us fall
to our knees on that alien "floor.")

(7) We touched nothing with bare hands.
Our gauntlets lugged the cases of gear,
deployed our probes and emblems,
set them prudently near the insect liftoff
station, with its flimsy ladder to home.

(8) All day it was night, the sky black
vacuum, though the strobe of the low sun
smote ferocious on that "loam."
We could not stoop, but scooped up
"clods" of the clinging "dust," that flowed
and glinted black, like "graphite."

(9) So, floating while trotting, hoping not
to stub our toe, we chose and catalogued
unearthly "rocks." These we stowed.

(10) And all night it was day, you could say,
with cloud-cuddled earth in the zenith,
a ghost moon that swiveled. The stars
were all displaced, or else were not
the ones we knew. Maneuvering by numbers
copied from head to head, we surveyed
our vacant outpost. Was it a "petrified
sea bed," inert "volcanic desert," or
crust over quivering "magma," that might
quake?

(11) It was possible to stand there.
And we planted a cloth "flower":
our country colors we rigged to blow
in the non-wind. We could not lift
our arms eye-high (they might deflate)
but our camera was a pistol, the trigger
built into the grip, and we took each
other's pictures, shooting from the hip.
Then bounced and loped euphoric,
enjoying our small weight.

(12) Our flash
eclipsed the sun at takeoff. We left our
insect belly "grounded," and levitated,
standing on its head. The dark dents
of our boots, unable to erode, mark how
we came: two white mechanic knights,
the first, to make tracks in some kind
of "sand." The footpads found it solid, so
we "landed." But that's not the right name.

Reprinted with the permission of
Simon & Schuster Books for Young Readers.

Name_____

First Walk on the Moon

Read the poem "First Walk on the Moon." Then answer the questions below.

1. In Stanza 1, how does the poet use metaphor to describe the moon-landing vehicle?

   _____

2. List four ways in which the poet refers to the moon.

   _____

3. In Stanza 3, what are the "thin fissures, of 'ink'"?

   _____

4. In Stanza 4, why does the poet put the word *soil* in quotes?

   _____

5. In Stanza 5, where is the literary form onomatopoeia used?

   _____

6. In Stanza 5, does the poet describe the moon as an inviting place? Explain your answer.

   _____

7. In what two ways does the poet use vivid imagery to describe the two astronauts?

   _____

8. How does Swenson describe the United States flag in the poem?

   _____

9. In Stanza 11, to what does "enjoying our small weight" refer?

   _____

10. Swenson uses quotes in this poem as a way to emphasize words. What words does she emphasize, and why?

   _____

   _____

Space Race (page 12)

Answers will vary.

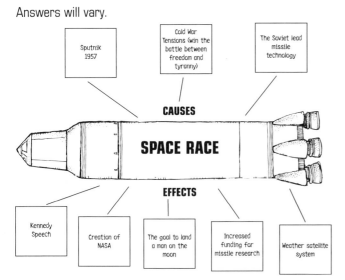

Sputnik 1957

Cold War Tensions (win the battle between freedom and tyranny)

The Soviet lead missile technology

CAUSES

SPACE RACE

EFFECTS

Kennedy Speech

Creation of NASA

The goal to land a man on the moon

Increased funding for missile research

Weather satellite system

Journalistic Writing Styles (page 17)

Inverted pyramids will vary.

Who: *Apollo 11* Commander Neil A. Armstrong
What: became the first person to walk on the moon
When: Sunday, July 20, 1969, 7:56 p.m., PDT
Where: on the surface of the moon
Why: to collect rocks that may reveal the oldest secrets of the solar system
How: via the spaceship *Eagle*

Newspaper Headlines (page 18)

Headlines will vary.
Extension Activity
Answers will vary.
All were explorers. They went places others had never gone before—unmapped. Mode of transportation and technological challenges.

The Front Page (page 19)

Front pages will vary.

Editorial Evaluation (page 23)

1. Hubert Humphrey
2. U. S. Senator of Minnesota
3. education; medicine; communications; weather forecasting; technological development in electronics; computers, and metallurgy
4. trained thousands of scientists, provided communication satellites, upgraded American industry and management, promoted international cooperation, contributed to national security and arms control agreements, given us pride and confidence as a people

"... And a Boomerang ..." (page 25)

1. c, 2. c, 3. b, 4. a, 5. d, 6. a

"Beyond Comfortable Horizons" (page 26)

1. d, 2. b, 3. b, 4. d
5. The cartoonist uses irony to show that the historic, near impossible mission to land a man on the moon and return him to earth safely, is in the end, easier than solving problems troubling average Americans right here on Earth.

"I Suppose It Was Inevitable!" (page 27)

1. moon rocks
2. as an unsavory character
3. The salesman is portrayed as dishonest.
4. No, the woman looks angry, and the remark is not positive.
5. Americans will make a commercial enterprise out of anything—Does anyone remember the Pet Rock craze?
6. Answers will vary.

First Walk on the Moon (page 30)

1. fabricated insect
2. mask of shadow, target, occult bloom, circle
3. our long shadows
4. Because, though the substance on the ground is where soil is found on Earth, it is so different that it cannot be called "soil."
5. ratatattat
6. No. They "saw no spore that any had stepped before," "not a thing has been born here, and nothing has died"—it was a dead and barren place.
7. Stanza 3—white twin uniforms, our heads transparent spheres, the outer visors gold
   Stanza 12—two white mechanic knights
8. a cloth flower
9. There is less gravitational pull on the moon, so a person's weight is about one-sixth of what it would be on Earth.
10. *Not ground, terrain, mare, grit, something like glass, soil, floor, loam, clods, dust, graphite, rocks, petrified sea bed, volcanic desert,* and *magma* are all terms that refer to Earth. She emphasized these words to highlight earthly descriptions for something that was not of Earth.

Teacher Resources

Arnold, H. J. P., ed. *Man in Space: An Illustrated History of Space Flight.* New York: Smithmark Publishers, Inc., 1993.

Baker, David. *The History of Manned Space Flight.* New York: Crown Publishers, Inc., 1981.

Gatland, Kenneth. *The Illustrated Encyclopedia of Space Technology.* New York: Orion Books, 1981, 1989.

Kennan, Erlend and Edmund H. Harvey, Jr. *Mission to the Moon: A Critical Examination of NASA and the Space Program.* New York: William Morrow & Co., Inc., 1969.

Matthews, Rupert. *Explorer.* New York: Alfred A. Knopf, 1991.

Ordway, Frederick I. III, Adams, Carsbie C., and Mitchell R. Sharpe. *Dividends from Space.* New York: Thomas Y. Crowell Company, 1971.

Ordway, Frederick I. III and Randy Lieberman. *Blueprint for Space: Science Fiction to Science Fact.* Washington, D.C.: Smithsonian Institution, 1992.

Ordway, Frederick I. III and Wernher Von Braun. *Space Travel: A History—An Update of History Rocketry and Space.* New York: Harper & Row Publishers, 1985.

Pellegrino, Charles R. and Joshua Stoff. *Chariots for Apollo: The Making of the Lunar Module.* New York: Atheneum, 1985.

Film Series

From the Earth to the Moon (HBO Studios, 1998). This six-episode made-for-television series follows the creation and explorations of the space program. Directed by Tom Hanks; 720 min.; VHS.

Student Resources

Gurney, Gene. *Americans to the Moon: The Story of Project Apollo.* New York: Random House, 1970.

Kerrod, Robin. *Race for the Moon.* Minneapolis, Minnesota: Lerner Publications Company, 1980.

Kramer, Barbara. *Neil Armstrong: The First Man on the Moon.* Springfield, New Jersey: Enslow Publishers, Inc., 1997.

Simon, Tony. *The Moon Explorers.* New York: Four Winds Press, 1970.

Vogt, Gregory. *Moon Landing and the Apollo: Missions in Space.* Brookfield, Connecticut: Millbrook Press, 1991.